United States Dept. of State

Return of the Whole Number of Persons

Within the Several Districts of the United States

United States Dept. of State

Return of the Whole Number of Persons
Within the Several Districts of the United States

ISBN/EAN: 9783337185985

Printed in Europe, USA, Canada, Australia, Japan

Cover: Foto ©ninafisch / pixelio.de

More available books at **www.hansebooks.com**

RETURN

NUMBER OF PERSONS

WITHIN THE

SEVERAL DISTRICTS

OF THE

UNITED STATES,

ACCORDING TO

"AN ACT PROVIDING FOR THE ENUMERATION OF THE
INHABITANTS OF THE UNITED STATES,"

PASSED MARCH THE FIRST,

ONE THOUSAND SEVEN HUNDRED AND NINETY-ONE.

———————

PRINTED BY CHILDS AND SWAINE.
M,DCC,XCI.

	1790	1800	1810	1820
Vermont	85 539			− 235 764
New Hampshire	141 885			‥ 244 161
Maine	96 540			− 298 335
Massacausetts	378,727	422.630	472 036	‥ 521 725
Rhode Island	− 68,825			83 059
Connecticut	‥ 237,946			− 275 242
New York	340,120	586 050	959.049	1,379 989
New Jersey	184.139			277 576
Pensylvania	‥ 434.373	602.545	810 091	1,046.844
Delaware	59 094			− − 72 749
Maryland	319,728			‥ 407 350
Virginia	747.610	880.200	974.622	1,028 623
N° Caroline	393.751			‥ 638 829
S° Caroline	−	‥	415 115	502,309
Georgia	‥ 82.548			340,989
Alabama				‥ 127 901
Mississipi				− 75 448
Louisiana				‥ 153 407
Tennesee				‥ 422 813
Kentucky	73.677			− − 564 317
Ohio				‥ 591.434
Indiana				147 178
Illinois				55 211
Missouri				66 581
Ter Michigan				− 8 891
Ter Arkansas				14 291

SCHEDULE of the whole Number of Persons within the several Districts of the United States, taken according to "An Act providing for the Enumeration of the Inhabitants of the United States;" passed March the 1st, 1790.

DISTRICTS.	Free white Males of sixteen years and upwards, including heads of families.	Free white Males under sixteen years.	Free white Females including heads of families.	All other free persons.	Slaves.	Total.
* Vermont	22,135	22,328	40,505	255	16	85,539
New-Hampshire	36,086	34,851	70,160	630	158	141,885
Maine	24,384	24,748	46,870	538	NONE	96,540 ⎱
Massachusetts	95,453	87,289	190,582	5,463	NONE	378,787 ⎰
Rhode-Island	16,019	15,799	32,652	3,407	948	68,825
Connecticut	60,523	54,403	117,448	2,808	2,764	237,946
New-York	83,700	78,122	152,320	4,654	21,324	340,120
New-Jersey	45,251	41,416	83,287	2,762	11,423	184,139
Pennsylvania	110,788	106,948	206,363	6,537	3,787	434,373
Delaware	11,783	12,143	22,384	3,899	8,887	59,094
Maryland	55,915	51,339	101,395	8,043	103,036	319,728
Virginia	110,936	116,135	215,046	12,866	292,627	747,610 ⎱
Kentucky	15,154	17,057	28,922	114	12,430	73,677 ⎰
North-Carolina	69,988	77,506	140,710	4,975	100,572	393,751
South-Carolina	-	-	-	-	-	-
Georgia	13,103	14,044	25,739	398	29,264	82,548

	Free white Males of twenty-one years and upwards, including heads of families.	Free Males under twenty-one years of age.	Free white Females, including heads of families.	All other Persons.	Slaves.	Total.
S. Western Territory	6,271	10,277	15,365	361	3,417	35,691
N. Do.	-	-	-	-	-	-

Truly stated from the original Returns deposited in the Office of the Secretary of State.

TH: JEFFERSON.

October 24. 1791.

* This return was not signed by the marshal, but was enclosed and referred to in a letter written and signed by him.

VERMONT.

		Free white males of 16 years and upwards, including heads of families.	Free white males under 16 years.	Free white females, including heads of families.	All other free persons.	Slaves.	Total.
ADDISON COUNTY.							
	Addison, - -	108	105	186	2		401
	Briftol, - -	53	57	101			211
	Bridport, - -	123	121	205			449
	Cornwall, - -	215	218	393			826
	Ferrifburg, - -	137	119	213	12		481
	Hancock, - -	18	11	27			56
	Kingfton, - -	26	31	44			101
TOWNS.	Leicefter, - -	94	81	168			343
	Middlebury, - -	125	92	176	2		395
	Monkton, - -	122	134	194			450
	Newhaven, - -	182	220	321			723
	Panton, - -	57	66	97			220
	Shoreham, - -	213	167	336	5		721
	Salifbury, - -	119	109	218			446
	Vergennes, - -	73	35	79	14		201
	Whiting, - -	70	57	122	1		250
	Weybridge, - -	49	41	84	1		175
		1784	1664	2964	31		6449
BENNINGTON COUNTY.							
	Arlington, - -	251	252	487		1	991
	Bennington, - -	639	604	1114	11	9	2377
	Bromley, - -	21	19	31			71
TOWNS.	Dorfett, - -	240	231	487			958
	Glaftonbury, - -	6	11	17			34
	Langrove, - -	7	4	20			31
	Manchefter, - -	338	338	595	2	3	1276
	Pownal, - -	419	499	825	2	1	1746
	Reedfborough, - -	16	16	32			64
	Rupert, - -	251	288	494			1033
	Shaftfbury, - -	491	530	974	3	1	1999

VERMONT.

	Free white males of 16 years and upwards, including heads of families.	Free white males under 16 years.	Free white females, including heads of families.	All other free persons.	Slaves.	Total.
BENNINGTON COUNTY. *Continued.*						
Stamford,	69	65	137	1		272
Sunderland,	113	101	199	1		414
Sandgate,	198	189	386			773
Woodford,	16	18	26			60
Windhall,	39	46	69		1	155
	3114	3211	5893	20	16	12254
CHITTENDEN COUNTY.						
Allburg,	147	106	189	4		446
Burlington,	108	70	151	3		332
Bolton,	21	26	41			88
Bakersfield,	4	4	5			13
Charlotte,	189	142	301	3		635
Cambridge,	108	84	167			359
Cambridge-gore,	3	6	6			15
Colchester,	42	40	55			137
Duxbury,	9	18	12			39
Elmore,	7	1	4			12
Essex,	118	76	160			354
Fairfax,	85	61	108			254
Fairfield,	46	28	55			129
Fletcher,	13	14	20			47
Georgia,	105	80	155			340
Hinesburg,	127	115	212			454
Highgate,	26	31	45	1		103
Huntsburg,	25	10	11			46
Hydespark,	10	12	18	3		43
Hungerford,	16	8	11	5		40
Isle-Mott,	18	13	16			47
Jerico,	115	90	176			381
Johnson,	31	16	46			93

VERMONT.

	Free white males of 16 years and upwards, including heads of families.	Free white males under 16 years.	Free white females, including heads of families.	All other free persons.	Slaves.	Total.
CHITTENDEN COUNTY. *Continued.*						
Milton, - -	90	65	127			282
Middlefex, - -	16	19	25			60
Moretown, - -	10	6	8			24
Minden, - -	6	6	6			18
Morriftown, - -	6		4			10
New-Huntington, -	34	40	62			136
New-Huntington-gore	10	7	14			31
North Hero, - -	40	25	57	3		125
Shelburne, - -	108	103	178			389
South Hero, - -	164	128	245			537
St. Albans, - -	89	61	105	1		256
Swanton, - -	22	25	27			74
Smithfield, - -	28	14	28			70
St. George, - -	14	17	26			57
Starkfborough, -	15	6	19			40
Underhill, - -	18	13	34			65
Waterbury, - -	22	27	44			93
Williſton, - -	136	120	215			471
Weſtford, - -	23	8	32			63
Waitsfield, - -	21	16	24			61
Wolcott, - -	11	7	14			32
	2256	1764	3258	23		7301
ORANGE COUNTY.						
Barnet, - -	137	132	207	1		477
Berlin, - -	38	33	63			134
Bradford, - -	159	176	312	7		654
Braintree, - -	61	66	89	5		221
Brookfield, - -	113	118	189	1		421
Brunfwick, - -	15	15	36			66
Cabot, - -	33	37	52			122

TOWNS.

VERMONT.

TOWNS.	ORANGE. COUNTY. Continued.	Free white males of 16 years and upwards, including heads of families.	Free white males under 16 years.	Free white females, including heads of families.	All other free persons.	Slaves.	Total.
	Calais, - -	14	11	20			45
	Canaan, - -	4	5	10			19
	Chelsea, - -	77	62	100			239
	Concord, - -	18	12	19			49
	Corinth, - -	147	156	275			578
	Danville, - -	165	139	270			574
	Dewey's-Gore, -	12	18	18			48
	Fairley, - -	132	120	210	1		463
	Greensborough, -	9	4	6			19
	Groton, - -	15	9	21			45
	Guildhall, - -	55	41	62			158
	Hardwich, - -	3					3
	Lemington, - -	12	7	12			31
	Littleton, - -	16	14	33			63
	Lunenburgh, -	30	29	60			119
	Lynden, - -	29	10	20			59
	Maidstone, - -	34	36	55			125
	Montpelier, - -	55	19	44			118
	Newbury, - -	225	223	413	12		873
	Northfield, - -	10	10	20			40
	Peachum, - -	102	90	173			365
	Randolph, - -	226	237	429			892
	Roxbury, - -	6	2	6			14
	Ryegate, - -	46	54	87			187
	Strafford, - -	214	228	403			845
	St. Johnsbury, -	54	34	55			143
	Thetford, - -	211	218	419	14		862
	Topsham, - -	36	56	70			162
	Tunbridge, - -	121	147	219			487
	Vershire, - -	117	118	204			439
	Walden, - -	3	3	5			11
	Walden's-Gore, -	9	9	14			32

VERMONT.

ORANGE COUNTY. Continued.	Free white males of 16 years and upwards, including heads of families.	Free white males under 16 years.	Free white females including heads of families.	All other free persons.	Slaves.	Total.
TOWNS						
Washington, - -	26	13	33			72
Wheelock, - -	14	7	12			33
Williamstown, -	41	34	71			146
Wilderfburg, -	30	16	30			76
	2874	2768	4846	41		10529

RUTLAND COUNTY.						
TOWNS						
Benfon, - -	185	182	290	1		658
Brandon, - -	154	168	314	1		637
Caftleton, - -	209	217	373	1		800
Clarenden, - -	343	397	738			1478
Chittenden, - -	38	49	72			159
Danby, - -	276	333	589	8		1206
Fair-Haven, - -	174	121	250			545
Hubberton, - -	120	94	190			404
Harwich, - -	38	49	78			165
Ira, - - -	77	82	153			312
Killington, - -	11	10	11			32
Midway, - -	7	9	18			34
Middletown, -	169	172	358			699
Orwell, - -	215	218	341	4		778
Pittsfield, - -	13	12	24			49
Philadelphia, - -	12	9	18			39
Poultney, - -	282	293	539	7		1121
Pittsford, - -	219	208	422	1		850
Pawlet, - -	348	399	709	2		1458
Rutland, - -	393	349	663	2		1407
Shrewfbury, - -	100	100	183			383
Sudbury, - -	67	69	122			258
Tinmouth, - -	247	244	442	2		935
Wallingford, - -	140	132	262	2		536
Wells, - -	149	176	297			622
	3986	4092	7450	31		15565

VERMONT.

	Free white males of 16 years and upwards, including heads of families.	Free white males under 16 years.	Free white females, including heads of families.	All other free persons.	Slaves.	Total.
WINDSOR COUNTY.						
Andover, - -	75	74	126			275
Barnard, - -	177	167	329			673
Bethel, - -	126	118	229			473
Bridgwater, - -	68	78	147			293
Cavendish, - -	126	125	240			491
Chester, - -	265	255	457	4		981
Hartford, - -	248	250	489	1		988
Hartland, - -	415	442	789	6		1652
Ludlow, - -	44	56	79			179
Norwich, - -	280	322	556			1158
Pomfret, - -	177	209	319	5		710
Reading, - -	171	211	359	6		747
Rochester, - -	62	47	106			215
Royalton, - -	195	190	363			748
Saltash, - -	29	35	42			106
Sharon, - -	147	147	275			569
Springfield - -	289	289	516	3		1097
Weathersfield, -	294	285	560	7		1146
Windsor, - -	395	406	732	9		1542
Stockbridge, -	32	25	43			100
Woodstock, - -	388	426	787	4		1605
	4003	4157	7543	45		15748
WINDHAM COUNTY.						
Athens, - -	103	138	209			450
Brattleborough, -	381	436	758	14		1589
Dummerston, -	363	394	734	10		1501
Guildford, - -	586	646	1187	13		2432
Hallifax, - -	302	342	661	4		1309
Hinsdale, - -	118	142	221	1		482
Jamacia, - -	71	66	126			263
Johnton's-Gore, -	15	13	21			49

VERMONT.

WINDHAM COUNTY. Continued.	Free white males of 16 years and upwards, including heads of families.	Free white males under 16 years.	Free white females, including heads of families.	All other free persons.	Slaves.	Total.
Londonderry,	90	99	172	1		362
Marlborough,	149	176	304			629
Newfane,	163	177	320			660
Putney,	438	492	906	12		1848
Rockingham,	327	319	587	2		1235
Somerſett,	26	35	50			111
Stratton,	27	22	46			95
Thomlinſon,	143	165	253			561
Townſhend,	192	171	313			676
Wardſboro' north diſt.	128	126	229			483
Wardſboro' ſouth diſt.	72	69	129			270
Weſtminſter,	430	387	783	1		1601
Whitingham,	114	119	209			442
Wilmington,	180	138	327			645
	4418	4672	8545	58		17693

(left margin: T O W N S.)

COUNTIES.	Free white males of 16 years and upwards, including heads of families.	Free white males under 16 years.	Free white females, including heads of families.	All other free persons.	Slaves.	Total.
Addiſon,	1784	1664	2964	37		6449
Bennington,	3114	3211	5893	20	16	12254
Chittenden,	2256	1764	3258	23		7301
Orange,	2874	2768	4846	41		10529
Rutland,	3986	4092	7456	31		15565
Windſor,	4003	4157	7543	45		15748
Windham,	4418	4672	8545	58		17693
Total,	22435	22328	40505	255	16	85539

NEW-HAMPSHIRE.

ROCKINGHAM COUNTY.	Free white males of 16 years and upwards including heads of families.	Free white males under 16 years.	Free white females, including heads of families.	All other free persons.	Slaves.	Total.
Portfmouth,	1158	973	2487	76	26	4720
Exeter,	437	343	859	81	2	1722
Gofport, on Star Ifland,	32	22	39			93
Greenland,	170	141	309	12	2	634
Rye,	226	189	439	8	3	865
Stratham,	229	158	486	8	1	882
Hampton Falls,	150	96	291	3	1	541
Hampton,	238	174	436	4	1	853
Northampton,	184	138	333	2		657
Newington,	132	109	285	2	14	542
Newcaftle,	125	117	292			534
Seabrook,	178	178	357	2		715
Newmarket,	284	235	610	7	1	1137
Brintwood,	255	224	490	6	1	976
Poplin,	137	103	251	1	1	493
Londonderry,	677	576	1339	24	6	2622
Southampton,	125	81	241	1		448
Plaftow,	135	129	257			521
Hampftead,	195	156	370	3		724
Atkinfon,	129	102	246	2		479
Kingfton,	243	189	471	3		906
Hawke,	101	94	224		1	420
Sandown,	138	115	308			561
Newtown,	126	132	271		1	530
Eaft-Kingfton,	90	87	179	2		358
Salem,	287	294	626	9	2	1218
Kenfington,	222	147	431			800
Deerfield,	452	358	806	1	2	1619
Nottingham,	275	249	529	4	11	1068
Loudon,	272	287	518	5	2	1084
Pittsfield,	214	221	449	4		888
Northwood,	188	181	374		1	744

TOWNS.

NEW-HAMPSHIRE.

ROCKINGHAM COUNTY. Continued.	Free white males of 16 years and upwards, including heads of families.	Free white males under 16 years.	Free white females, including heads of families.	All other free persons.	Slaves.	Total.
Epsom, - -	200	175	424			799
Epping, - -	318	254	654	2	5	1233
Northfield, - -	154	155	295	2		606
Canterbury, -	285	223	526	1	3	1038
Chichester, -	137	118	236			491
Pembrook, -	240	245	469		2	956
Concord, - -	505	408	823	7	4	1747
Bow, - -	149	151	268			568
Allenstown, -	67	63	123	1		254
Chester, - -	494	447	960	1		1902
Candia, - -	246	273	521			1040
Pelham, - -	216	190	385			791
Raymond, -	177	181	361	8		727
Windham, - -	156	173	328	1	5	663
	11148	9654	21976	293	98	43169
STRAFFORD COUNTY.						
Dover, - -	549	419	1004	18	8	1998
Somersworth, -	248	211	478		6	943
Rochester, -	730	740	1386		1	2857
New-Durham, -	139	140	275			554
Middleton, -	151	162	304			617
Wolfborough, -	110	120	217			447
Moultonborough,	133	148	283		1	565
Sandwich, -	216	243	446			905
Ossipee, - -	86	82	171			339
Wakefield, -	158	193	295			646
Tuftonborough,	29	20	60			109
Tamworth, -	67	72	126		1	266
Barnstead, -	192	214	400		1	807
Eaton, - -	60	72	121			253

NEW-HAMPSHIRE.

	Free white males of 16 years and upwards, including heads of families.	Free white males under 16 years.	Free white females, including heads of families.	All other free persons.	Slaves.	Total.
STRAFFORD COUNTY. *Continued.*						
Effingham, -	42	43	68		1	154
Conway, -	149	146	279			574
Durham, -	336	272	634	2	3	1247
Barrington, -	605	646	1217	2		2470
Madbury, -	167	126	295	4		592
Lee, -	277	224	526	2		1029
New-DurhamGore,	108	118	212	7		445
Sanborntown,	415	423	749			1587
New-Hampton,	171	173	306	2		652
Meridith, -	247	211	419	4		881
Gilmantown, -	614	682	1294	22	1	2613
Stark's & Sterling's Locations	12	13	26			51
	6011	5913	11591	63	22	23601
CHESHIRE COUNTY.						
Charlestown, -	307	254	530	1	1	1093
Keene, -	318	318	671	5	2	1314
Acworth, -	159	197	348			704
Alstead, -	268	285	558			1111
Chesterfield, -	441	532	930	2		1905
Claremont, -	348	391	692	2	2	1435
Cornish, -	238	258	484	1	1	982
Croydon, -	121	151	262	3		537
Dublin, -	227	223	446	5		901
Fitzwilliam, -	255	278	505			1038
Gilsom, -	70	64	164			298
Hinsdale, -	127	142	251		2	522
Jaffrey, -	285	336	603	11		1235
Langdon, -	58	76	108	2		244
Lempster, -	110	95	207	3		415
Marlborough,	175	219	392			786

NEW-HAMPSHIRE.

	Free white males of 16 years and upwards, including heads of families.	Free white males under 16 years.	Free white females, including heads of families.	All other free persons.	Slaves.	Total.
CHESHIRE COUNTY. *Continued.*						
Marlow, - -	73	80	160			313
Newport, -	187	198	390	4	1	780
Packersfield, -	167	208	343	3		721
Richmond, -	332	368	680			1380
Rindge, -	276	306	554	7		1143
Stoddard, -	162	194	344		1	701
Surry, - -	117	111	220			448
Sullivan, -	48	68	103	1		220
Swanzey, -	293	287	571	6		1157
Unity, - -	133	139	265	1		538
Walpole, -	327	335	580	1	2	1245
Washington, -	137	135	273			545
Wendell, -	70	64	133			267
Westmoreland,	472	543	998	4	1	2018
Winchester, -	298	311	595	4	1	1209
New-Grantham,	90	88	153	1	1	333
Plainfield, -	259	277	486	2		1024
Protectworth, -	56	49	104		1	210
	7004	7580	14103	69	16	28772
HILLSBOROUGH COUNTY.						
Amherst, -	571	576	1204	18		2369
Duxbury Mile-flip,	39	45	85			169
Bedford, - -	210	240	440	8		898
Derryfield Gore, -	10	4	16			30
Wilton, - -	253	278	562	12		1105
Dunstable, -	179	146	306	1		632
Nottingham West,	267	246	544	7		1064
New-Ipswich, -	338	285	614	4		1241
Merimack, - -	209	207	393	10		819
Hillsborough, -	193	211	393	1		798

TOWNS. (CHESHIRE)

TOWNS. (HILLSBOROUGH)

NEW-HAMPSHIRE.

HILLSBOROUGH COUNTY. Continued.	Free white males of 16 years and upwards, including heads of families.	Free white males under 16 years.	Free white females, including heads of families.	All other free persons.	Slaves.	Total.
Goffstown, -	324	303	614	34		1275
Litchfield, - -	97	83	160	17		357
Newboston, -	313	303	576	10		1202
Antrim, - -	138	146	244			528
Heniker, - -	269	325	525	8		1127
Peterborough, -	220	214	423	4		861
Fisherfield, - -	68	105	158			331
Lyndborough, -	313	349	618			1280
Lyndborough-Gore	11	8	19			38
Bradford, - -	56	60	101			217
Sutton, - -	132	122	266			520
New-London, -	69	90	152			311
Warner, - -	220	195	448			863
Kiarserge-Gore, -	27	27	49			103
Andover, - -	166	167	312			645
Boscawen, - -	282	274	551	1		1108
Society, - -	84	89	146			319
Hancock, - -	156	160	315	3		634
Sharon, - -	68	63	128			259
Campbell's Gore,	28	35	57			120
Salisbury, - -	345	385	640	2		1372
Temple, - -	177	196	368	6		747
Mason, - -	215	242	462	3		922
Raby, - - -	86	89	160	3		338
Weare, - -	491	500	931	2		1924
Hopkinton, - -	445	417	852	1		1715
Francestown, - -	232	233	517			982
Dunbarton, - -	209	244	444	20		917
Dearing, - -	213	254	459	2		928
Hollis, - -	340	378	723			1441
Derryfield, - -	92	95	175			362
	8155	8389	16150	177		32871

NEW-HAMPSHIRE.

GRAFTON COUNTY.	Free white males of 16 years and upwards, including heads of families.	Free white males under 16 years.	Free white females, including heads of families.	All other free persons.	Slaves.	Total.
Haverhill, -	163	118	266	1	4	552
Plymouth, -	182	142	297		4	625
Alexandria, -	79	87	132			298
Bartlett, - -	55	57	135		1	248
Bath, - -	117	136	239		1	493
Bridgewater, -	84	62	134		1	281
Burton, - -	34	45	62			141
Cambridge not inhabited						
Campton, -	113	79	202		1	395
Canaan, - -	137	123	223			483
Chatham, -	17	13	28			58
Cockburne, -	9	5	12			26
Cockermouth, -	94	104	175			373
Colburne, -	10	6	13			29
Concord alias Gunthwaite	91	75	147			313
Coventry, -	21	20	47			88
Dalton, - -	3	4	7			14
Dartmouth, -	34	25	52			111
Dorchester, -	48	45	82			175
Dummer, not inhabited,						
Enfield alias Relhan	188	173	361	2		724
Errol, not inhabited,						
Franconia, -	22	18	32			72
Grafton, -	99	110	194			403
Hannover, including 152 Students at Dart. Coll.	476	298	596	8	2	1380
Kilkenny, not inhabited,						
Lancaster, -	45	45	71			161
Landaff, - -	75	80	137			292
Lebanon, -	375	282	515	8		1180
Lincoln, - -	8	5	9			22
Littleton, -	28	26	42			96
Lyman, - -	57	39	106			202

C

NEW-HAMPSHIRE.

	GRAFTON COUNTY. Continued.	Free white males of 16 years and upwards, including heads of families.	Free white males under 16 years.	Free white females, including heads of families.	All other free persons.	Slaves.	Total.
TOWNS.	Lyme, - -	231	189	392	4		816
	Milfield, not inhabited,						
	New-Chester, -	70	103	139			312
	New-Holdernefs,	96	73	160			329
	Northumberland,	34	27	56			117
	Orange, - -	32	37	61	1		131
	Orford, -	140	125	272		3	540
	Peeling, not inhabited,						
	Percy, - -	14	11	23			48
	Piermont, - -	103	113	206	1	3	426
	Rumney, - -	97	113	201			411
	Shelburne, -	12	5	18			35
	Stratford, - -	44	38	64			146
	Succefs, not inhabited,						
	Thornton, -	96	98	191			385
	Trecothick not inhabited						
	Warren, - -	52	64	86	4		206
	Wentworth, -	56	73	112			241
LOCATIONS.	Hales's, -	3	2	4			9
	Dame's, -	4	8	9			21
	Hart's, -	3	4	5			12
	Senter's, -	5		3			8
	Stark's, -	8	5	16			29
	Sterling's, -	3	2	4			9
	Wales's, -	1	3	2			6
		3768	3315	6340	28	21	13472

NEW HAMPSHIRE.

COUNTIES.	Free white males of 16 years and upwards, including heads of families.	Free white males under 16 years.	Free white females, including heads of families.	All other free persons.	Slaves.	Total.
Rockingham, -	11148	9654	21976	293	98	43169
Strafford, - -	6011	5913	11591	63	23	23601
Cheshire, -	7004	7580	14103	69	16	28772
Hillsborough, -	8155	8389	16150	177		32871
Grafton, -	3768	3315	6340	28	21	13472
	36086	34851	70160	630	158	141885

DISTRICT OF NEW-HAMPSHIRE,

Portsmouth, *August* 10th, 1791.

JOHN PARKER, Marshal.

MAINE.

YORK COUNTY.		YORK COUNTY. *Continued.*	
Kittery -	3250	Limrick -	411
York - -	2900	Waterborough	965
Wells -	3070	Coxhall -	775
Arundel -	1458	Sanford -	1802
Biddeford -	1018	Fryſburgh -	547
Pepperellborough	1352	Brownfield *and* }	
Little Falls -	607	Suncook }	250
Little Oſſepee	662	Waterford *and* }	
Berwick -	3894	Penecook }	250
Lebanon -	1275	New-Andover, }	
Shapleigh -	1329	Hiram *and* }	214
Waſhington	262	Porterfield }	
Parſonſield -	655	Buxton -	1564
Franciſborough	311		28821

MAINE.

TOWNS.	CUMBERLAND COUNTY.		LINCOLN COUNTY. Continued.	
	Portland -	2240	Bowdoinham	455
	Gorham -	2244	Nobleborough	516
	Scarborough	2235	Waldoborough	1210
	Falmouth -	2991	Briftol -	1718
	Cape Elizabeth	1355	Cufhing -	942
	New-Glocefter	1358	Warren -	646
	Grey -	577	Thomafton -	801
	Windham	938	Meduncook	322
	Otisfield -	197	Union -	200
	Raymondtown	345	Winthrop -	1240
	Bridgton -	329	Balltown -	1072
	Flintftown -	190	Bowdoin -	983
	Standifh -	716	Vaffalborough	1240
	Butterfield -	189	Jones' Plantation	262
	Ruffield -	448	Lewiftown -	532
	Turner -	349	Fairfield -	492
	Bucktown -	453	Prefcott & Carr's Plantation	159
	Shepherdfield	530	Sandy River No. 2	130
	Bakerftown -	1276	Sandy River No. 1	494
	North Yarmouth	1978	Sandy River No. 3	350
	Freeport -	1330	Hancok -	278
	Durham -	724	Winflow -	779
	Brunfwick -	1387	Canaan -	454
	Harpfwell -	1071	Norridgwalk -	376
		25450	Titcomb -	264
	LINCOLN COUNTY.		Karatunk -	103
	Pownalborough	2055	Sandy River No. 4	327
	Woolwich -	797	Little River -	64
	Georgetown	1333	Smithtown -	521
	Bath -	949	Wales -	439
	Topfham -	826	Green -	639
	Boothbay -	997	New-Sandwich	297
	Edgcomb -	855	Wafhington -	618
	New-Caftle -	896	Sterling -	166
	Pittfton -	605	Rockymekoe	103
	Hallowell -	1194	Littleborough	263
				29962

M A I N E.

HANCOCK COUNTY. TOWNS.		WASHINGTON COUNTY. TOWNS.	
Penobſcott -	1048	Machias -	818
Vinalhaven -	578	Plantations eaſt of Machias, No. 1 }	66
Deer Iſle -	682	No. 2 -	144
Eaſtern River	240	No. 4 -	54
Buckſtown -	316	No. 5 -	84
Orrington -	477	No. 8 -	244
Edeſton -	110	No. 9 -	29
Conduſkeeg -	567	No. 10 -	42
Frankfort -	891	No. 11 -	37
Mount-Deſert	744	No. 12 -	54
Goldſborough	267	No. 13 -	7
Sullivan -	504	Plantations weſt of Machias, No. 4 }	233
Trenton -	312	No. 5 -	177
Townſhip No. 6	239	No. 6 -	208
Bluehill -	274	No. 11 -	95
Sedgwick -	569	No. 12 -	8
Belfaſt -	245	No. 13 -	223
Ducktrap -	278	No. 22 -	175
Canaan -	132	Buckharbour	61
Barretſtown -	173		2758
Camden -	331		
Iſleſborough	382		
Orphan-Iſland	124		
Small Iſlands	66		
	9549		

C O U N T I E S.

York, -		28,821
Cumberland, -		25,450
Lincoln, -		29,962
Hancock, -		9,549
Waſhington, -		2,758
Total, -		96,540

HENRY DEARBORN,
Marſhal of Maine Diſtrict.

MASSACHUSETTS.

To Col. Samuel Bradford of Bofton, - - 9 Towns and the Iflands in the harbour of Bofton.

Col. John Steele Tyler of Roxbury, - 14
— The whole of Suffolk county, 23

Mr. William Ingalls of New-buryport, - 9
Mr. B. Stevens of Salem, 9
Mr. J. Wingate of Haverhill, 4 North of Merimack river in — Effex county.
The whole of Effex county, 22
The above mentioned Wingate 1½ North of the Merrimack in Middlefex county.

Maj. Aaron Brown of Groton, 19
Brig. Gen. Henry Woods of Pepperell, - 20½
— The whole of Middlefex county 41

Maj. Gen. William Shepherd of Weftfield, - 33 on the weft fide of Connecticut River.
Hon. D. Sexton of Deerfield, 27 on the eaft fide of faid river, — and Deerfield befides.
The whole of Hampfhire county 60
Hon. J. Thomas of Plymouth, The whole of Plymouth county 15
Capt. J. Thomas of Plymouth, The whole of Barnftable county 10
The laft mentioned Thomas, The ifland counties of Dukes county and Nantucket, 4
Hon. David Cobb of Taunton, The whole of Briftol county, 15
Maj. B. Kimbal of Harvard, 17 Towns and gores adjoining.
Mr. P. Fofter of Brookfield, 16 Do.   do.
Mr. J. Paine of Worcefter, 16
— The whole of Worcefter county 49

Henry W. Dwight, Efq. of Stockbridge, - 14 Towns, gores, &c. adjoining.
Mr. Thomas Allen, jun. of Pittsfield, - 12 Do.   do.
— The whole of Berkfhire county, 26

265

N. B. The faid Diftrict of Maffachufetts (not comprehending the old Province of Maine) contains but eleven counties; in which are two hundred and fixty-five towns, befides fome few diftricts, gores of land, plantations, &c. not incorporated, and iflands upon the fea coaft; the inhabitants of all which are included in the following enumeration.

MASSACHUSETTS.

New (handwritten)

SUFFOLK COUNTY. S. Bradford's return.	Number of houses.	Number of families.	Free white males of 16 years and upwards.	Free white males under 16 years.	Free white females.	All other free persons.	Total of each town.	
Boston	2376	3343	4325	3376	9576	761	18038	24937
Roxbury	287	351	617	459	1110	40	2826	
Brookline	61	68	152	94	225	13	484	
Dorchester	256	311	488	345	859	30	1722	
Milton	153	184	271	205	536	27	1039	
Hingham 1659	337	411	505	454	1102	24	2085	
Cohaffet	126	159	188	212	417		817	
Hull	21	25	24	31	63	2	120	
Chelfea	60	81	134	95	222	21	472	
Iflands in the harbour of Boston	15	15	192	19	66	5	282	
	3692	4948	6896	5290	14176	923	27285	
J. S. Tyler's return.								
Bellingham	106	121	187	184	362	2	735	
Braintree	420	488	687	640	1426	18	2771	
Dedham	255	288	438	360	845	16	1659	
Dover	82	90	120	112	249	4	485	
Foxborough	109	117	165	169	340		674	
Franklin	155	186	305	235	558	3	1101	
Medway	159	187	282	210	522	21	1035	
Medfield	114	129	201	120	395	15	731	
Needham	167	208	277	274	566	13	1130	
Sharon	161	189	256	258	515	5	1034	
Stoughton	315	356	484	477	1012	21	1994	
Walpole	145	175	256	250	494	5	1005	
Wrentham 1804	243	278	471	387	907	2	1767	2061
Weymouth	232	278	346	368	747	8	1469	
Total of J. S. Tyler's return,	2663	3090	4475	4044	8938	133	17590	
S. Bradford's.	3692	4948	6896	5290	14176	923	27285	
Total of Suffolk,	6355	8038	11371	9334	23114	1056	44875	
ESSEX COUNTY. W. Ingall's return.								
Newburyport	616	939	1155	1071	2541	70	4837	5946
Newbury	538	728	1039	844	2047	42	3971	4056
Gloucefter	673	1006	1267	1216	2793	41	5317	5313
Apfwich 2673	601	881	1151	916	2416	79	4562	3305
Andover 3853	402	525	743	612	1414	94	2863	2741

MASSACHUSETTS.

	Number of houses.	Number of families.	Free white males of 16 years and upwards.	Free white males under 16 years.	Free white females.	All other free persons.	Total of each town.
ESSEX COUNTY. *Continued.* 1820 W. Ingall's return.							
Rowley -	278	328	453	366	94	9	1772
Bradford -	196	253	378	263	725	5	1371
Boxford -	128	163	247	191	481	6	925
Topsfield -	107	150	213	156	398	13	780
	3539	4968	6646	5635	13759	359	26399
1820 B. Steven's return.							
Salem 12.791 -	928	1493	1845	1710	4106	260	7921
Marblehead -	618	1104	1265	1327	2982	87	5661
Beverly 4283 -	422	637	748	733	1751	58	3290
Danvers -	372	460	626	486	1279	34	2425
Lynn -	300	404	625	514	1132	20	2291
Manchester	142	196	234	204	518	9	965
Middleton -	102	119	164	140	362	16	682
Wenham -	74	92	114	109	269	10	502
Lynnfield -	66	82	119	108	261	3	491
	3024	4587	5740	5331	12660	497	24228
J. Wingate's return of the towns in Essex north of the Merrimack.							
Salisbury 2006 -	267	325	458	381	931	10	1780
Almsbury -	303	351	470	384	944	3	1801
Haverhill 3074	330	435	611	539	1251	7	2408
Methuen -	181	217	338	292	663	4	1297
Total of J. Wingate's,	1081	1328	1877	1596	3789	24	7286
W. Ingall's,	3539	4968	6646	5635	13759	359	26399
B. Stevens's,	3024	4587	5740	5331	12660	497	24228
Total of Essex,	7644	10883	14263	12562	30208	880	57913
MIDDLESEX COUNTY. A. Brown's return.							
Cambridge 3295		355	535	454	1066	60	2115
Lincoln -		125	180	184	370	6	740
Concord -		293	415	314	832	29	1590
Bedford -		89	150	117	254	2	523
Billerica -		217	335	256	595	5	1191
Medford -		187	260	215	520	34	1029
Woburn -		326	452	397	855	23	1727

MASSACHUSETTS.

	Number of houses.	Number of families.	Free white males of 16 years and upwards.	Free white males under 16 years.	Free white females.	All other free persons.	Total of each town.
MIDDLESEX COUNTY. *Continued.* 1820 A. Brown's return.							
Chelmsford -		209	327	233	572	12	1144
Reading 2797 -		341	480	386	905	31	1802
Tewkfbury -		163	239	229	483	7	958
Charleftown or 41		288	395	354	809	25	1583
Waltham -		141	234	208	430	10	882
Watertown -		164	319	250	511	11	1091
Carlifle -		96	149	99	305	2	555
Weftford -		220	301	306	618	4	1229
Wilmington -		134	181	172	345	18	710
Groton -		322	477	429	929	5	1840
Malden -		193	239	214	560	20	1033
Stoneham -		72	108	83	182	8	381
	3183	3935	5776	4900	11141	306	22123
82 H. Wood's return.							
Pepperell -	164	209	286	245	581	20	1132
Townfend -	145	185	273	244	472	4	993
Shirley -	99	115	166	155	354	2	677
Dunftable -	59	67	107	79	193	1	380
Afhby -	110	122	187	194	369	1	751
Boxborough -	51	67	100	86	217	9	412
Marlborough	218	288	425	340	781	8	1554
Lexington -	135	176	251	212	470	8	941
Eaft-Sudbury -	112	144	206	176	410	9	801
Sudbury -	175	240	326	287	675	2	1290
Acton -	120	140	216	204	427	6	853
Natick -	75	113	142	134	300	39	615
Littleton -	121	159	223	177	438	16	854
Framingham 2087	221	292	394	350	828	26	1598
Sherburn -	92	150	211	192	392	6	801
Hopkinton -	169	220	311	329	665	12	1317
Hollifton -	95	150	237	199	424	15	875
Newton -	175	237	336	301	698	25	1360
Stow -	130	145	206	195	397	3	801
Wefton -	132	173	256	227	504	23	1010
Tyngfborough on weft fide Merimack	31	35	52	46	87	17	202
	2629	3427	4911	4372	9682	252	19217

D

MASSACHUSETTS.

	Number of houses.	Number of families.	Free white males of 16 years and upwards.	Free white males under 16 years.	Free white females.	All other free persons.	Total of each town.
MIDDLESEX COUNTY. Continued. J. Wingate's return.							
Tyngsborough on north side Merimack	26	32	43	50	87		180
Dracut -	160	186	310	284	584	39	1217
Total of J.Wingate's,	186	218	353	334	671	39	1397
A. Brown's,	3183	3935	5776	4900	11141	306	22123
H. Woods's,	2629	3427	4911	4372	9682	252	19217
Total of Middlesex,	5998	7580	11040	9606	21494	597	42737
HAMPSHIRE COUNTY. W. Shepherd's return.							
Northampton -	242	259	498	341	771	18	1628
Easthampton -	75	77	127	108	221	1	457
Southampton -	130	135	226	178	418	7	829
Westhampton -	101	102	163	185	333	2	683
West-Springfield	372	384	630	525	1160	52	2367
Hatfield -	103	110	199	147	343	14	703
Greenfield -	224	240	391	390	714	3	1498
Westfield -	326	348	527	565	1054	58	2204
Whately -	120	130	184	199	352	1	736
Williamsburgh	159	173	258	261	520	10	1049
Granville -	319	334	496	501	969	13	1979
Colerain -	229	245	348	371	687	11	1417
Worthington -	181	188	287	277	547	5	1116
Goshen -	102	103	161	185	327	8	681
Shelburne -	169	184	300	273	598	12	1183
Conway -	306	321	500	558	1021	13	2092
Blandford -	235	239	345	359	703	9	1416
Bernardston -	101	108	176	172	343		691
Leyden -	150	155	208	298	481	2	989
Charlemont -	106	110	166	173	326		665
Chester -	177	187	285	300	527	7	1119
Chesterfield -	180	190	283	317	581	2	1183
Ashfield -	243	261	354	369	735	1	1459
Southwick -	123	148	215	217	397	12	841
Norwich -	126	129	187	199	352	4	742
Montgomery -	72	74	110	116	221	2	449
Cummington -	140	148	237	212	419	5	873
Plainfield -	81	85	109	120	224	5	458
Middlefield -	97	101	155	173	280		608

MASSACHUSETTS.

		Number of houses.	Number of families.	Free white males of 16 years and upwards.	Free white males under 16 years.	Free white females.	All other free persons.	Total of each town.
TOWNS.	**HAMPSHIRE COUNTY.** *Continued.* *W. Shepherd's return.*							
	Buckland -	119	124	164	191	363		718
	Rowe -	76	79	119	122	202		443
	Heath -	58	58	86	105	188		379
	Plantation No. 7	88	90	134	156	249		539
		5330	5619	8628	8663	16626	277	34194
	D. Sexton's return.							
TOWNS.	Deerfield -	181	191	354	306	646	24	1330
	Springfield 1414	238	266	415	359	787	13	1574
	Long Meadow -	119	126	200	182	356	6	744
	Hadley -	132	143	240	187	436	19	882
	South-Hadley -	113	118	209	181	359	10	759
	Sunderland -	73	74	123	101	237	1	462
	Montague -	150	154	236	217	451	2	906
	Northfield -	120	122	224	224	415	5	868
	Wilbraham -	223	230	382	393	755	25	1555
	Amherst -	176	183	335	287	609	2	1233
	Granby -	93	100	164	154	276	2	596
	Brimfield -	172	178	318	309	582	2	1211
	South-Brimfield	98	99	144	171	291		606
	Holland -	65	66	115	97	204	12	428
	Ludlow -	86	94	134	158	266	2	560
	Monion -	188	194	336	324	653	18	1331
	Palmer -	117	125	215	186	396	12	809
	Belchertown -	238	240	370	396	713	6	1485
	Greenwich -	171	174	271	265	504	5	1045
	Pelham -	153	159	246	277	517		1040
	Leverett -	86	87	126	129	268	1	524
	Shutesbury -	117	117	160	196	315	3	674
	Wendell -	79	80	130	147	242		519
	Ware -	116	116	189	205	378	1	773
	Warwick -	176	179	279	308	657	2	1246
	New-Salem 1446	254	261	390	387	765	1	1543
	Orange	117	122	186	203	395		784
Total of D. Sexton's.		3851	3998	6491	6349	12473	174	25487
W. Shepherd's.		5330	5619	8628	8663	16626	277	34194
Total of Hampshire,		9181	9617	15119	15012	29099	451	59681

MASSACHUSETTS.

TOWNS	PLYMOUTH COUNTY. 1820 Joshua Thomas's return.	Number of houses.	Number of families.	Free white males of 16 years and upwards.	Free white males under 16 years.	Free white females	All other free persons.	Total of each town.
	Plymouth 4348 -		577	749	646	1546	54	2995
	Middleborough 4587		802	1166	1050	2286	24	4526
	Pembroke -		341	480	433	998	43	1954
	Carver - -		150	214	214	407	12	847
	Plympton - -		163	233	220	499	4	956
	Halifax - -		124	178	155	329	2	664
	Duxborough -		258	278	322	744	10	1454
	Wareham -		135	202	208	434	10	854
	Hanover - -		184	268	235	546	35	1084
	Abington -		255	359	339	740	15	1453
	Bridgewater 5650 -		830	1259	1123	2470	129	4975
	Scituate 3206 -		521	692	554	1545	65	2856
	Marshfield -		225	386	210	645	28	1269
	Rochester 1074		442	681	605	1304	54	2644
	Kingston -		166	261	220	505	18	1004
	Total of Plymouth,	4240	5173	7500	6534	14998	503	29535
	BRISTOL COUNTY. David Cobb's return.							
	Taunton 4520 -	538	661	924	862	1928	90	3804
	Norton - -	195	245	376	309	730	13	1428
	Easton - -	207	261	366	379	704	17	1466
	Mansfield -	147	175	271	198	509	5	983
	Attleborough 3057	314	384	566	451	1131	18	2166
	Swanzey .. -	246	329	430	369	913	72	1784
	Somerset -	141	189	270	234	585	62	1151
	Dighton - -	236	285	416	409	879	89	1793
	Raynham -	164	197	300	222	543	29	1094
	Berkley -	119	139	213	179	447	11	850
	Freetown -	298	362	565	465	1117	55	2202
	Westport 2633 -	365	452	615	536	1259	56	2466
	Dartmouth, 3636	392	448	645	540	1231	83	2499
	New-Bedford 3747	454	582	856	726	1693	38	3313
	Rehoboth 2740 -	688	832	1151	1063	2405	91	4710
	Ten more houses reported afterwards	10						
	Total of Bristol,	4514	5541	7964	6942	16074	729	31709

MASSACHUSETTS.

	Number of houses.	Number of families.	Free white males of 16 years and upwards.	Free white males under 16 years.	Free white females.	All other free persons.	Total of each town.
BARNSTABLE COUNTY. *J. Thomas's return, Deputy Marshal.*							1320
Barnstable 3324 -		481	631	623	1301	55	2610
Falmouth		217	418	365	816	38	1637
Sandwich 2232 -		263	460	469	1015	47	1991
Yarmouth -		450	651	667	1327	33	2678
Harwich -		420	545	593	1243	11	2392
Eastham -		311	426	431	974	3	1834
Wellfleet -		210	301	252	562	2	1117
Chatham -		196	267	292	578	3	1140
Truro -		221	324	279	586	4	1193
Province-Town		95	142	99	211	2	454
Plantation of Marshpee		25	35	27	72	174	308
Total of Barnstable.	2343	2880	4200	4097	8685	372	17354
DUKES COUNTY AND NANTUCKET.							
Edgarton -		221	336	318	682	16	1352
Tisbury -		204	287	239	609	7	1142
Chilmark -		133	199	157	405	10	771
Total of Dukes County,		558	822	714	1696	33	3265
Nantucket County or Town of Sherburne,		872	1193	1016	2301	110	4620
Total of Dukes County and Nantucket,	1013	1430	2015	1730	3997	143	7885	7255
WORCESTER COUNTY. *John Paine's return.*							
Worcester 1952 -		322	601	494	949	51	2095
Ward -		74	128	118	227		473
Gerry -		120	178	182	379	1	740
Paxton -		108	140	139	271	8	558
Boylstone -		111	226	183	415	15	839
Shrewsbury -		156	269	209	473	12	963
Athol -		133	219	205	419	5	848
New-Braintree -		124	254	188	483	14	939
Rutland -		186	295	243	526	8	1072
Leicester -		179	286	245	537	8	1076
Barre . .		297	426	401	748	38	1613
Petersham .		302	397	377	781	5	1560
Holden .		204	278	267	532		1077

MASSACHUSETTS.

WORCESTER COUNTY. *Continued.* 1820 *J. Paine's return.*	Number of houses	Number of families	Free white males of 16 years and upwards	Free white males under 16 years	Free white females	All other free persons	Total of each town
TOWNS.							
Sutton		624	671	662	1297	12	2642
Oakham		112	191	197	383	1	773
Grafton		162	241	210	421		872
	2998	3214	4800	4320	8841	178	18139
P. Foster's return.							
Berlin	81	93	129	138	245		512
Hardwick	245	282	460	394	858	13	1723
Dudley	159	183	267	278	557	12	1114
Douglafs	165	200	267	264	548		1079
Sturbridge	228	263	445	400	855	4	1704
Weftern	124	142	247	227	414	11	899
Brookfield 2292	438	504	784	762	1547	7	3100
Charlton	298	344	502	490	971		1965
Spencer	192	220	338	316	662	6	1332
Oxford	148	165	272	236	487	5	1000
Uxbridge	179	218	344	311	636	17	1308
Mendon	222	265	388	369	795	3	1555
Upton	126	155	211	199	394	29	833
Northbridge	83	96	137	140	287	5	569
Milford	135	164	225	175	427	12	839
Gardner	85	90	121	156	253	1	534
In the gore adjoining Oxford	33	39	53	61	123		237
In the gore adjoining Sturbridge	10	10	15	20	29		64
	2951	3433	5205	4936	10088	127	20356
B. Kimbal's return.							
Lancafter	214	257	387	313	737	23	1460
Sterling	209	248	377	350	687	14	1428
Harvard	198	249	362	298	716	11	1387
Lunenburgh	192	229	302	310	663	2	1277
Leominfter	166	190	314	254	613	8	1189
Fitchburgh	166	181	265	300	585	1	1151
Weftminfter	177	195	310	277	585	4	1176
Royalfton	166	192	275	282	571	2	1130
Princeton	144	159	258	251	504	3	1016
Afhburnham	146	161	212	261	469	9	951
Winchendon	149	158	239	250	455	2	946
Templeton	134	152	232	226	492		950

MASSACHUSETTS.

	Number of houses.	Number of families.	Free white males of 16 years and upwards.	Free white males under 16 years.	Free white females.	All other free persons.	Total of each town.
WORCESTER COUNTY. *Continued.* **B. Kimbal's return.**							
Hubbardston	138	154	221	257	440	15	933
Bolton	125	148	238	173	449	1	861
Westborough	118	144	240	258	432	4	934
Southborough	124	154	205	189	442	1	837
Northborough	88	101	161	152	302	4	619
In the gore adjoining Leominster	4	4	5	10	12		27
In the gore adjoining Fitchburgh	2	2	2	6	6		14
In the gore adjoining Princeton	4	4	5	6	15		26
Total of B. Kimbal's,	2664	3082	4610	4423	9175	104	18312
J. Paine's,	2998	3214	4800	4320	8841	178	18139
P. Foster's,	2951	3433	5205	4936	10088	127	20356
Total of Worcester,	3613	9729	14615	13679	28104	409	56807
BERKSHIRE COUNTY. **H. W. Dwight's return.**							
Stockbridge		198	311	322	639	64	1336
West Stockbridge		178	260	298	545	10	1113
Lee		203	286	310	571	3	1170
Becket		127	195	187	362	7	751
Loudon		62	96	84	164		344
Tyringham		236	337	368	683	9	1397
Great Barrington		221	328	335	664	46	1373
Alford		98	142	173	262		577
Egremont		122	187	191	376	5	759
Mount Washington		43	57	78	126		261
Sheffield		330	470	463	934	32	1899
New Marlborough		253	395	400	742	13	1550
Sandisfield		258	382	380	810	9	1581
Bethlehem		48	62	73	125	1	261
South 11000 acres adjoining Sandisfield		27	37	43	81		161
Boston Corner adjoining Mount Washington		12	13	21	33		67
	2207	2416	3558	3726	7117	199	14600

TOWNS.

MASSACHUSETTS.

TOWNS. 1820 BERKSHIRE COUNTY. T. Allen junr's return.	Number of houses.	Number of families.	Free white males of 16 years and upwards.	Free white males under 16 years.	Free white females.	All other free persons.	Total of each town.
Lanesborough		346	522	547	1058	15	2142
Adams		325	473	560	1003	4	2040
Pittsfield 2763.		312	497	496	957	45	1992
Williamstown		270	445	454	865	5	1769
Richmond		176	336	291	624	4	1255
Lenox		181	279	299	574	17	1169
Hancock		190	297	325	588	1	1211
Partridgefield		172	250	279	500	3	1041
Windsor		151	222	233	454	7	916
Washington		96	143	160	283	2	588
Dalton		94	129	134	283	8	554
New Ashford		78	92	126	240	2	460
In the gore adjoining Adams & Windsor		73	102	121	191	11	425
In the gore adjoining Williamstown		7	8	22	21		51
Total of T. Allen jun.	2257	2471	3792	4047	7650	124	15613
H. W. Dwight's	2207	2416	3558	3726	7117	199	14600
Zoar, a plantation returned by W. Shepherd	12	12	16	20	42		78
Total of Berkshire,	4476	4899	7366	7793	14809	323	30291

COUNTIES IN THE DISTRICT OF MASSACHUSETTS.	Number of towns.	Number of houses.	Number of families.	Free white males of 16 years old and upwards.	Free white males under 16 years.	Free white females.	All other free persons.	Slaves.	Total of each county.
Suffolk,	23	6,355	8,038	11,371	9,334	23,114	1,056	—	44,875
Essex,	22	7,644	10,883	14,263	12,562	30,208	880	—	57,913
Middlesex,	41	5,998	7,580	11,040	9,606	21,494	597	—	42,737
Hampshire,	60	9,181	9,617	15,119	15,012	29,099	451	—	59,681
Plymouth,	15	4,240	5,173	7,500	6,534	14,998	503	—	29,535
Bristol,	15	4,514	5,541	7,964	6,942	16,074	729	—	31,709
Barnstable,	10	2,343	2,889	4,200	4,097	8,685	372	—	17,354
Dukes County,	3 }	1,013	558 }	822	714	1,696	33	—	3,265
Nantucket,	1		872	1,193	1,016	2,301	110	—	4,620
Worcester,	49	8,613	9,729	14,615	13,679	28,104	409	—	56,807
Berkshire,	26	4,476	4,899	7,366	7,793	14,809	323	—	30,291
Eleven Counties.	265	54,377	65,779	95,453	87,289	190,582	5,463	None.	378,787

A Copy, examined.

JONA. JACKSON,
Marshal of the district of Massachusetts.

F

RHODE-ISLAND.

		Free white males of 16 years and upwards, including heads of families.	Free white males under 16 years.	Free white females, including heads of families.	All other free persons.	Slaves.	Total in each town.	Total in each county.
NEWPORT COUNTY.								
TOWNS.	Newport	1454	1237	3385	417	223	6716	14,300.
	Portsmouth	373	346	777	47	17	1560	
	New-Shoreham	155	133	290	57	47	682	
	James-Town	100	91	232	68	16	507	
	Middletown	214	161	424	26	15	840	
	Tiverton	570	520	1161	177	25	2453	
	Little Compton	365	354	778	22	23	1542	
PROVIDENCE COUNTY.								
TOWNS.	Providence	1709	1259	2937	427	48	6380	24,391.
	Smithfield	818	682	1583	83	5	3171	
	Scituate	562	548	1170	29	6	2315	
	Glocester	989	999	2014	22	1	4025	
	Cumberland	501	485	970	8		1964	
	Cranston	444	408	942	73	10	1877	
	Johnston	333	280	633	71	3	1320	
	North-Providence	270	237	509	50	5	1071	
	Foster	528	602	1119	15	4	2268	
WASHINGTON COUNTY.								
TOWNS.	Westerly	460	679	1081	68	10	2298	18,075.
	North-Kingstown	602	668	1342	199	96	2907	
	South-Kingstown	820	1058	1605	473	175	4131	
	Charlestown	344	445	815	406	12	2022	
	Exeter	583	613	1175	87	37	2495	
	Richmond	366	510	815	67	2	1760	
	Hopkinton	521	678	1184	72	7	2462	
BRISTOL COUNTY.								
TOWNS.	Bristol	330	291	677	44	64	1406	3,211.
	Warren	286	243	555	16	22	1122	
	Barrington	165	144	330	32	12	683	
KENT COUNTY.								
TOWNS.	Warwick	566	516	1152	224	35	2493	8,848.
	East-Greenwich	426	393	920	72	13	1824	
	West-Greenwich	520	586	913	20	10	2054	
	Coventry	645	633	1159	35	5	2477	
		16019	15799	32652	3407	948	68825	

WILLIAM PECK, Marshal.

CONNECTICUT.

COUNTIES.	Free white males of 16 years and upwards.	Free white males under 16 years.	Free white females.	All other free persons.	Slaves.	Total.
Hartford	9782	8840	18714	430	263	38029
New-Haven	7856	6858	15258	425	433	30830
New-London	8224	7183	16478	729	586	33200
Fairfield	9187	8398	17541	327	797	36250
Windham	7440	6551	14406	340	184	28921
Litchfield	10041	9249	18909	323	233	38755
Middlesex	4730	4132	9632	140	221	18855
Tolland	3263	3192	6510	94	47	13106
	60523	54403	117448	2808	2764	237946

PHILIP B. BRADLEY, *Marshal*
for the District of Connecticut.

NEW-YORK.

	Free white males of 16 years and upwards, including heads of families.	Free white males under 16 years.	Free white females, including heads of families.	All other free persons.	Slaves.	Aggregate total.	More females than males.	More males than females.
RICHMOND COUNTY.								
Castle Town	178	173	314	26	114	805		37
Westfield	197	223	427	31	276	1151	7	
Southfield	151	129	306	35	234	855	26	
Northfield	223	226	402	35	135	1021		47
Total,	749	751	1449	127	759	3835	33	84
KINGS COUNTY.								
Brooklyn	362	257	565	14	405	1603		54
Flatbush	160	153	238	12	378	941		75
New-Utrecht	98	81	167	10	206	562		12
Gravesend	88	69	129	5	135	426		28
Flatlands	72	71	143		137	423		
Bushwick	123	69	172	5	171	540		20
Total,	903	700	1414	46	1432	4495		189
QUEENS COUNTY.								
New-Town	420	353	753	52	533	2111		20
Jamaica	397	294	697	65	222	1675	6	
Flushing	325	229	590	123	340	1607	36	
N. Hampstead	550	442	1026	171	507	2606	34	
Oyster-Bay	949	756	1709	302	381	4097	4	
S. Hampstead	913	789	1705	95	326	3828	3	
Total,	3554	2863	6480	808	2309	16014	83	20
SUFFOLK COUNTY.								
Huntington	763	742	1468	74	213	3260		37
Islip -	132	126	248	68	35	609		10
Smith Town	195	179	369	113	166	1022		5
Brookhaven	727	617	1372	275	233	3224	28	
Shelter-Island	39	38	77	23	24	201		
Southhold	765	646	1436	190	182	3219	25	
S. Hampton	781	653	1544	284	146	3408	110	
E. Hampton	354	272	673	99	99	1497	47	
Total,	3756	3273	7187	1126	1098	16440	210	52

TOWNS.

NEW-YORK.

TOWNS.	NEW-YORK CITY and COUNTY.	Free white males of 16 years and upwards, including heads of families.	Free white males under 16 years.	Free white females including heads of families.	All other free persons.	Slaves.	Aggregate total.	More females than males.	More males than females.
TOWNS.	City of N.York	8328	5797	14963	1060	2180	32328	838	
	Harlem Division	172	110	291	41	189	803	9	
	Total.	8500	5907	15254	1101	2369	33131	847	
	WEST-CHESTER COUNTY.								
TOWNS.	Morriffina .	43	17	41	2	30	133		19
	Weft-Chefter	217	212	421	49	242	1203		70
	Eaft-Chefter	174	160	320	11	75	740		14
	Pelham .	45	31	84	1	38	199	8	
	Yonkers .	265	220	458	12	170	1125		27
	Greenburgh	330	323	616	9	122	1400		37
	New-Rochelle	170	130	277	26	89	692		23
	Scarfdale -	73	53	113	14	28	281		13
	Momaroneck	108	98	171	18	57	452		35
	Rye .	258	164	427	14	123	986	5	
	Harrifon .	242	220	453	35	54	1004		9
	White-Plains	130	100	218	8	49	505		12
	Mt. Pleafant	501	422	909	8	84	1924		14
	North-Caftle	608	593	1205	43	29	2478	4	
	Bedford .	618	622	1182	10	38	2470		58
	Poundridge	247	270	538	7		1062	21	
	Salem .	366	326	728	14	19	1453	36	
	North-Salem	266	239	509	16	28	1058	4	
	Stephen .	343	297	612	7	38	1297		28
	York .	389	381	771	28	40	1609	1	
	Cortlandt .	484	452	905	25	66	1932		31
	Total,	5939	5330	10958	357	1419	24003	79	390
	DUTCHESS COUNTY.								
TOWNS.	Frederickftown	1437	1540	2851	41	63	5932		126
	Phillipftown	517	593	942	2	25	2079		168
	Southeaft-Town	231	241	433	3	13	921		39
	Pawling .	1031	1068	2098	91	42	4330		1
	Beekman .	847	951	1682	11	106	3597		116
	Fifhkill .	1366	1290	2643	41	601	5941		13
	Poughkeepfie	617	573	1092	48	199	2529		98
	Clinton .	1173	1112	2115	31	176	4603		170
	Amenia .	768	780	1449	29	52	5078		99

G

NEW-YORK.

		Free white males of 16 years and upwards, including heads of families.	Free white males under 16 years.	Free white females, including heads of families.	All other free persons.	Slaves.	Aggregate total.	More females than males.	More males than females.
TOWNS.	**DUTCHESS** COUNTY. Continued.								
	Northeaſt-Town	839	863	1597	22	80	3401		105
	Rhynebeck	875	756	1514	66	421	3662		87
	Waſhington	1267	1295	2494	55	78	5189		68
	Total,	10968	11062	20940	440	1856	45266		1090
TOWNS.	**ORANGE** COUNTY.								
	Miniſink .	552	546	1049	17	51	2215		49
	Goſhen .	616	519	1012	59	212	2448		93
	New-Cornwall	1081	1029	1906	42	167	4225		204
	Warwick .	869	896	1702	41	95	3603		63
	Haverſtraw .	1191	1174	2207	16	238	4826		158
	Orange-Town	291	176	470	26	203	1175	12	
	Total,	4600	4340	8385	201	966	18492	12	567
TOWNS.	**ULSTER** COUNTY.								
	Woodſtock .	278	268	453	11	15	1025		93
	Middletown	293	259	460	1	6	1019		92
	Rocheſter .	374	321	638	14	281	1628		57
	Mama-Cating	436	491	780	5	51	1763		147
	Hurly .	166	129	306	1	245	847	11	
	Marbletown .	492	469	840	15	374	2190		121
	Shawangunk	484	453	821	20	350	2128		116
	Montgomery .	898	834	1578	17	236	3563		154
	Wallkill .	604	690	1166	8	103	2571		128
	New-Windſor	463	417	805	17	117	1819		75
	New-Burgh .	615	590	1091	12	57	2365		114
	New-Marlboro'	536	605	1027	15	58	2241		114
	New-Paltz .	513	520	962	12	302	2309		71
	Kingſton .	906	745	1558	9	711	3929		93
	Total,	7058	6791	12485	157	2906	29397	11	1375
TOWNS.	**COLUMBIA** COUNTY.								
	Canan-Town	1713	1704	3235	5	35	6692		182
	Hills-Dale	1054	1220	2245	6	31	4556		29
	Livingſton	1101	1112	2148		233	4594		65
	Kinderhook	1035	1028	1954	6	638	4661		109
	Claverack	744	749	1418	11	340	3262		75

	Free white males of 16 years and upwards, including heads of families.	Free white males under 16 years.	Free white females, including heads of families.	All other free persons.	Slaves.	Aggregate total.	More females than males.	More males than females.
COLUMBIA COUNTY. Continued.								
Hudfon	618	590	1156	27	193	2584		52
Clermont	190	207	357		113	867		40
German-Town	118	127	231		40	516		14
Total,	6573	6737	12744	55	1623	27732		566
ALBANY COUNTY.								
Ranffelaerwick town	2027	2086	3635		570	8318		478
Stephen-Town	1713	1832	3224	1	25	6795		321
Balls-Town	1890	2022	3329	23	69	7333		583
Cambridge .	1242	1308	2405		41	4996		145
Half-Moon .	843	954	1670	7	128	3602		127
Saratoga .	738	868	1404	8	53	3071		202
Hofack .	693	841	1456	18	27	3035		78
Still-Water .	770	794	1436	10	61	3071		128
Eafton ..	568	724	1199		48	2539		93
Pitts-Town .	566	700	1148		33	2447		118
Schachticoke .	409	387	694		343	1833		102
Scheneẞady	180	170	328		78	756		22
On iflands not included in towns.	6	8	9		6	29		5
Albany City	804	653	1443	26	572	3498		14
Water-Vliet	1737	1696	3262	17	707	7419		171
Coxakie .	800	812	1474	8	302	3406		148
Katts-kill .	475	357	835	8	305	1980	3	
Freehold .	530	425	861	1	5	1822		94
Ranffelaer-Ville	707	740	1311		13	2771		136
Duanelburgh	410	369	865	1	5	1470		94
Schohary .	542	435	936	8	152	2073		41
Schenectady S. of the Mowhawk.	899	675	1483	34	381	3472		91
Total,	18549	18866	34227	170	3924	75736	3	3191
MONTGOMERY COUNTY.								
Otefgo .	563	427	698	6	8	1702		292
Caughnewaga	1128	1068	1928	4	133	4261		268
Palatine .	805	815	1582	10	192	3404		38
Mowhawk	1088	1141	2092	8	111	4440		137
German-Flatts	354	301	630	2	20	1307		25

NEW-YORK.

	Free white males of 16 years and upwards, including heads of families.	Free white males under 16 years.	Free white females, including heads of families.	All other free persons.	Slaves.	Aggregate total.	More females than males.	More males than females.
MONTGOMERY COUNTY. *Continued.*								
TOWNS. Herkermer .	406	388	722	1	8	1525		72
Whites-Town .	689	443	749	3	7	1891		383
Chemung .	648	644	1091	1	7	2391		201
Connafoxharrie	1648	1538	2868	6	96	6156		318
Harpersfield .	524	424	772		6	1726		176
Chenango .	13	12	20			45		5
Total,	7866	7201	13152	41	588	28848		1915
WASHINGTON COUNTY.								
TOWNS. Salem-Town .	581	561	1021	1	22	2186		121
Granville .	583	564	1093			2240		54
Argvle .	624	646	1057		14	2341		213
Weſtfield .	544	591	959		9	2103		176
Hebron .	406	479	818			1703		67
Queenſberry	261	275	543		1	1080	7	
Kingſberry .	299	291	529	1		1120		61
Whitehall .	209	214	381	1	1	806		42
Hampton .	108	131	224			463		15
Total,	3615	3752	6625	3	47	14042	7	749
CLINTON COUNTY.								
TOWNS. Champlain-Town	188	125	247	15	3	578		66
Plattſburgh	153	108	184		13	458		77
Wellſburgh .	132	86	156		1	375		62
Crown-Point	73	38	91	1		203		20
Total,	546	357	678	16	17	1614		225
Ontario County.	524	192	342	6	11	1075		374

NEW-YORK.

Summary of the Totals of the different Counties.

	Free white males of 16 years and upwards, including heads of families.	Free white males under 16 years.	Free white females, including heads of families.	All other free persons.	Slaves.	Aggregate total.	More females than males.	More males than females.
Richmond	749	751	1449	127	759	3835		51
Kings	903	700	1414	46	1432	4495		189
Queens	3554	2863	6480	808	2309	16014	63	
Suffolk	3756	3273	7187	1126	1098	16440	158	
N. York city &co.	8500	5907	15254	1101	2369	33131	847	
West-Chester	5939	5330	10958	357	1419	24003		311
Dutchess	10968	1062	20940	440	1856	45266		1090
Orange	4600	4340	8385	201	966	18492		555
Ulster	7058	6791	12485	157	2906	29397		1364
Columbia	6573	6737	12744	55	1623	27732		566
Albany	18549	18866	34227	170	3924	75736		3188
Montgomery	7866	7201	13152	41	588	28848		1915
Washington	3615	3752	6625	3	47	14042		742
Clinton	546	357	678	16	17	1614		225
Ontario	524	192	342	6	11	1075		374
Total,	83700	78122	152320	4654	21324	340120	1068	10570

NEW-YORK, July 26th, 1791.

W. S. SMITH.

	Free white males of 16 years and upwards, including heads of families.	Free white males under 16 years.	Free white females, including heads of families.	All other free persons.	Slaves.	Total number.	Total number in each county.
HUNTERDON COUNTY. TOWNS.							
Amwell	1249	1173	2480	16	283	5201	
Kingwood	603	574	1161	4	104	2446	
Hopewell	579	448	1041	19	233	2320	
Trenton	498	346	841	79	182	1946	
Alexandria	377	401	685	0	40	1503	20,253.
Bethleham	331	329	643	1	31	1335	
Maidenhead	237	189	432	14	160	1032	
Lebanon							
Readington							
Tewkſbury	1092	919	2033	58	268	4370	
SUSSEX COUNTY. TOWNS.							
Greenwich	507	510	944	10	64	2035	
Oxford	471	468	892	9	65	1905	
Mansfield	377	368	700	2	35	1482	
Knowlton	488	490	935	11	13	1937	
Sandyſton	131	122	239	1	26	519	
Wantage	459	437	777	1	26	1700	19,500.
Hardyſton	610	637	1110	10	26	2393	
Montague	150	124	241	3	25	543	
Wallpack	129	102	233	2	30	496	
Newton							
Independance							
Hardwicke	1641	1681	3023	16	129	6490	
BURLINGTON COUNTY. TOWNS.							
Cheſterfield							
Notingham							
Little-Eggharbor							
Eveſham							
New-Hanover							
Cheſter	4625	4164	8481	598	227	18095	18,095.
Springfield							
Northampton							
Mansfield							
Burlington							
Willingborough							
ESSEX COUNTY. TOWNS.							
Newark							
Acquacknack	4339	3972	8143	160	1171	17785	17,785.
Elizabethtown							

NEW-JERSEY.

	Free white males of 16 years and upwards, including heads of families.	Free white males under 16 years.	Free white females, including heads of families.	All other free persons.	Slaves.	Total number.	Total number in each county.
MONMOUTH COUNTY.							
TOWNS. Middletown	711	618	1343	62	491	3225	
Upper-Frehold	763	789	1532	108	250	3442	
Lower-Frehold	819	778	1549	12	627	3785	16,918
Stafford	219	221	441		2	883	
Dover	237	231	422	6	14	910	
Shrewsbury	1094	1041	2161	165	212	4673	
MORRIS COUNTY.							
TOWNS. Pequanack							
Roxbury							
Morristown	4092	3938	7502	48	636	16216	16,216
Hanover							
Mendham							
MIDDLESEX COUNTY.							
TOWNS. Amboy	149	108	246	31	48	582	
Woodbridge	871	774	1587	32	256	3520	
Piscataway	537	514	982	10	218	2261	
North-Brunswick	638	456	1010	3	205	2312	15,956
South-Brunswick	439	361	789	10	218	1817	
South-Amboy	642	597	1196	8	183	2626	
Windsor	719	565	1318	46	190	2838	
GLOUCESTER COUNTY.							
TOWNS. Waterford							
Newtown							
Gloucester township							
Gloucester town							
Deptford	3287	3311	6232	342	191	13363	13,363
Greenwich							
Woolwich							
Eggharbor							
Galloway							
BERGEN COUNTY.							
TOWNS. New-Barbadoes							
Bergen							
Hackinsack							
Harrington	2865	2299	4944	192	2301	12601	12,601
Franklin							
Saddle River							

NEW-JERSEY.

	Free white males of 16 years and upwards, including heads of families.	Free white males under 16 years.	Free white females including heads of families.	All other free persons.	Slaves.	Total number.	Total number in each county.
SOMERSET COUNTY.							
Bridgewater .	586	462	1119	34	377	2578	12,296.
Bedminſter .	275	260	489	4	169	1197	
Bernardſtown .	601	560	1115	8	93	2377	
Eaſtern-Precinct	481	298	795	26	468	2068	
Weſtern-Precinct	413	345	744	56	317	1875	
Hillſborough .	463	465	868	19	386	2201	
SALEM COUNTY.							
Mannington .							10,437.
Salem							
Elſingborough .							
Lower-Alloways Creek							
Upper-Alloways Creek	2679	2396	4816	374	172	10437	
Pitts-Grove							
Piles-Grove .							
Upper-Penn's Neck							
Lower-Penn's Neck							
CUMBERLAND COUNTY.							
Greenwich .							8,248.
Hopewell .							
Stowenuk .							
Deerfield .	2147	1966	3877	138	120	8248	
Fairfield .							
Downs .							
Maurice River .							
CAPE-MAY COUNTY.							
Upper-Precinct .							2,571.
Lower-Precinct .	631	609	1176	14	141	2571	
Middle-Precinct .							
	45251	41416	83287	2762	11423	184139	

DISTRICT of NEW-JERSEY, *the 2d of April* 1791.

THOMAS LOWREY, Marſhal.

PENNSYLVANIA.

Counties.	Free white males of 16 years and upwards, including heads of families.	Free white males under 16 years.	Free white females, including heads of families.	All other free persons.	Slaves.	Total.
Philadelphia City of Philadelphia	7739	5270	13883	1420	210	28522
Suburbs	3621	2974	6955	385	63	13998
Total of city & suburbs	11360	8244	20838	1805	273	42520
Remainder of Philad. county	3126	2652	5682	297	114	11871
Montgomery	6008	5383	10984	440	114	22929
Bucks	6575	5947	12037	581	261	25401
Delaware	2536	2113	4495	289	50	9483
Chester	7488	6595	13166	543	145	27937
Lancaster	9713	8070	17471	545	348	36147
Berks	7714	7551	14648	201	65	30179
Northampton	6008	6410	11676	133	23	24250
Luzerne	1236	1331	2313	13	11	4904
Dauphin	4657	4437	8814	57	212	18177
Northumberland	4191	4726	8046	109	89	17161
Mifflin	1954	1949	3558	42	59	7562
Huntingdon	1872	2089	3537	24	43	7565
Cumberland	4821	4537	8456	206	223	18243
Bedford	2887	3841	6316	34	46	13124
Franklin	4022	3860	7170	273	330	15655
York	9213	9527	17671	837	499	37747
Westmoreland	4013	4355	7483	39	128	16018
Allegany	2635	2745	4761	9	159	10300
Washington	5334	7170	11087	12	263	23866
Fayette	3425	3416	6154	48	282	13325
Total,	110788	106948	206363	6537	3737	434373

Philadelphia, August 19th, 1791.

CLEMENT BIDDLE, *Marshal*
in and for *Pennsylvania District.*

I

DELAWARE.

COUNTIES.	Free white males of 16 years and upwards, including heads of families.	Free white males under 16 years.	Free white females, including heads of families.	All other free persons.	Slaves.	Total.
New-Castle	3973	4747	7767	639	2562	19686
Kent	3705	3467	6878	2570	2300	18920
Suffex	4105	3929	7739	690	4025	20488
	11783	12143	22384	3899	8887	59094

Amounting in the whole to fifty-nine thoufand and ninety-four perfons within the faid diftrict.

A. M'LANE, *Marfhal*
Delaware Diftrict.

DELAWARE DISTRICT, May 4, 1791.

MARYLAND.

COUNTIES & TOWNS.	Free white males of 16 years and upwards.	Free white males under 16 years.	Free white females of all ages.	All other free persons.	Slaves.	Total.
WESTERN SHORE.						
Harford County	2872	2812	5100	775	3417	14976
Baltimore County	5184	4668	9101	604	5877	25434
Baltimore Town & Precincts	5866	2556	5503	323	1255	13503
Ann-Arundel County	3142	2850	5672	804	10130	22598
Frederick County .	7010	7016	12911	213	3641	30791
Allegany County .	1068	1283	2188	12	258	4809
Washington County	3738	3863	6871	64	1286	15822
Montgomery County	3284	2746	5649	294	6030	18003
Prince George County	2653	2503	4848	164	11176	21344
Calvert County .	1091	1109	2011	136	4305	8652
Charles County .	2565	2399	5160	404	10085	20613
St. Marys County	2100	1943	4173	342	6985	15544
	38573	35748	69187	1136	64445	212089
EASTERN SHORE.						
Cæcil County .	2847	2377	4831	163	3407	13625
Kent County	1876	1547	3325	655	5433	12836
Queen Anns County	2158	1974	4039	618	6674	15463
Caroline County .	1812	1727	3489	421	2057	9506
Talbot County .	1938	1712	3581	1076	4777	13084
Somersett County	2185	1908	4179	268	7070	15610
Dorchester County	2541	2430	5039	528	5337	15875
Worcester County	1985	1916	3725	178	3836	11640
	55915	51339	101395	8043	103036	319728

VIRGINIA.

Names of Counties.	Names of Assistants.	Free white males of 16 years and upwards.	Free white males under 16 years.	Free white females.	All other free persons.	Slaves.	Total.
Augusta, the part east of the north mountain	R. Porterfield	2048	1665	3138	40	1222	} 10886
Part west of do.	C. Cameron	551	572	986	19	345	
Albemarle	James Kerr	1703	1790	3342	171	5579	12585
Accomack	R. Tunford	2297	2177	4502	721	4262	13959
Amherst	C. Kenny	2056	2235	3995	121	5296	13703
Amelia, including Nottoway a new county	Charles Jones	1709	1697	3278	106	11307	18097
Botetourt, as it stood previous to the formation of Wythe from it & Montg'ry.	Joseph Paxton	2247	2562	4432	24	1259	10524
Buckingham	G. Bernard	1274	1537	2685	115	4168	9779
Berkley	N. Orrick	4253	4547	7850	131	2932	19713
Brunswick	John Stith	1472	1529	2918	132	6776	12827
Bedford	D. Sanders	1785	2266	3674	52	2754	10531
Cumberland	P.I. Carrington	885	914	1778	142	4434	8153
Chesterfield	A. Graves	1652	1557	3149	369	7487	14214
Charlotte	Jacob Morton	1285	1379	2535	63	4816	10078
Culpeper	T. C. Fletcher	3372	3755	6682	70	8226	22105
Charles-City	R. Goodrich	532	509	1043	363	3141	5588
Caroline	Henry Chiles	1799	1731	3464	203	10292	17489
Campbell	R. Hunter	1236	1347	2363	251	2488	7685
Dinwiddie	J. R. Davis	1790	1396	2853	561	7334	13934
Essex	T. Banks	908	869	1766	139	5440	9122
Elizabeth-City	R. Saunders	390	388	778	18	1876	3450
Fauquier	S. Morgan	2674	2983	5500	93	6642	17892
Fairfax	T. Pollard	2138	1872	3601	135	4574	12320
Franklin	Thomas Hale	1266	1629	2840	34	1073	6842
Fluvanna	J. Johnston	589	654	1187	25	1466	3921
Frederick division	Edward Smith	1757	1653	3041	49	1319	} 19681
Ditto	John Smith	2078	2517	4269	67	2931	
Gloucester	W. Camp	1597	1523	3105	210	7063	13498
Goochland	R. H. Saunders	1028	1059	2053	257	4656	9053
Greensville	J. Peterson	669	627	1234	212	3620	6362
Greenbrier, including Kanawa a new county	W. Johnson	1463	1574	2639	20	319	6015
Henrico	Z. Rowland	1823	1170	2607	581	5819	12000
Hanover	J.M. Walker	1637	1412	3242	240	8223	14754
Hampshire	F. Taggart	1662	1956	3261	13	454	7346
Harrison	W. Martin	487	579	947		67	2080

VIRGINIA.

Names of Counties.	Names of Assistants.	Free white males of 16 years and upwards.	Free white males under 16 years.	Free white females.	All other free persons.	Slaves.	Total number.
Hardy	W. Bullet	1108	2256	3192	411	369	7336
Halifax	W. M'Craw	2214	2320	4397	226	5565	14722
Henry	R. Payne	1523	1963	3277	165	1551	8479
Isle of Wight	T. Fearn	1208	1163	2415	375	3867	9028
James City	R Saunders	395	359	765	146	2405	4070
King William	W. Winston	723	732	1438	84	5151	8128
King & Queen	John Bagby	995	1026	2138	75	5143	9377
King George	W.H.Parker	757	781	1585	86	4157	7366
Lunenburg	John Ballard	1110	1185	2251	80	4332	8959
Loudon	S. D. Hariman	3677	3992	7080	183	4030	18962
Lancaster	Joseph Carter	535	542	1182	143	3236	5638
Louisa	C.Yancey, Jun.	957	1024	1899	14	4573	8467
Mecklenburg	John Ballard	1857	2015	3683	416	6762	14733
Middlesex	T. Churchill	407	370	754	51	2558	4140
Monongalia	J. Dougherty	1089	1245	2168	12	154	4768
Montgomery, as it stood previous to the formation of Wythe from it and Botetourt	James Newell	2846	3744	5804	6	828	13228
Norfolk	John Ingram	2650	1987	4291	251	5345	14524
Northampton	James Palmer	857	743	1581	464	3244	6889
New-Kent	W. Graves	605	587	1190	148	2700	6239
Northumberland	Joseph Locke	1046	1137	2323	197	4460	9153
Nansemond	John Bell	1215	1167	2331	480	3817	9010
Orange	J. Wood, Jun	1317	1426	2693	64	4421	9921
Ohio	R. Woods	1222	1377	2308	24	281	5212
Prince Edward	Charles Jones	1044	1077	1961	32	3986	8100
Prince William	W. Grayson	1644	1797	3303	167	4704	11615
Prince George	J. R. Davies	965	822	1600	267	4519	8173
Powhatan	P.I. Carrington	683	548	1115	211	4325	6822
Pendleton	C. Cameron	568	686	1124	1	73	2452
Pittsylvania	W. M'Craw	2008	2447	4083	62	2979	11579
Princess Anne	J. Ingram	1169	1151	2207	64	3202	7793
Richmond	W. H. Parker	704	697	1517	83	3984	6985
Randolph	John Elliott	221	270	441		19	951
Rockingham	L. Yauncey	1816	1652	3209		772	7449
Russell	C. Carter	734	969	1440	5	190	3338
Rockbridge	John M'Kee	1517	1552	2756	41	682	6548
Spotsylvania	John Fox	1361	1278	2532	148	5933	11252
Stafford	S. Payton	1341	1355	2769	87	4036	9588
Southampton	James Gee	1632	1546	3134	559	5993	12864
Surry	I.G.Adkins	732	651	1379	368	3097	6227
Shannandoah	W. Jennings	2409	2779	4791	19	512	10510
Sussex	David Mason	1215	1174	2382	391	5387	10554

VIRGINIA.

Names of Counties	Names of Assistants.	Free white males of 16 years and upwards.	Free white males under 16 years.	Free white females.	All other free persons.	Slaves.	Total.
Warwick	R. Saunders	176	158	333	33	990	1690
Walhington	W. Preston	1287	1440	2440	8	450	5625
Westmoreland	W. H. Parker.	815	754	1614	114	4425	7722
York	R. Saunders	530	461	1124	358	2760	5233
		110936	116135	215046	12866	292627	747610

Principal Towns, the Inhabitants whereof being included in the general Return.

Names of the towns.	In what Counties situated.	Free white males of 16 years and upwards.	Free white males under 16 years.	Free white females.	All other free persons.	Slaves.	Total.
Alexandria	Fairfax	734	480	939	52	543	2748
Frederickfburg	Spottylvania	318	187	354	59	567	1485
Richmond	Henrico	878	353	786	265	1479	3761
Petersburg in Dinwiddie comprehending Blandford in Prince George & Pocahun·as in Chesterfield		583	205	465	310	1265	2828
Williamsburg	James City & York	186	108	368	46	636	1344
Borough of Norfolk	Norfolk	599	312	693	61	1294	2959
Portsmouth	do.	294	209	536	47	616	1702
Winchester	Frederick	464	341	664	12	170	1651
York	York	68	56	148	17	372	61

Amounting to one hundred and ten thousand nine hundred and thirty-six free white males of 16 years and upwards—One hundred and sixteen thousand one hundred and thirty-five free white males under 16 years—Two hundred and fifteen thousand and forty-six free white females—Twelve thousand eight hundred and sixty-six other free persons—And two hundred and ninety-two thousand six hundred and twenty-seven slaves. Total seven hundred and forty-seven thousand six hundred and ten.

EDWARD CARRINGTON,
Marshal of the District of Virginia.

KENTUCKY.

Free white males of 16 years and upwards, including heads of families.	Free white males under 16 years.	Free white females, including heads of families.	All other free persons.	Slaves.	Total.
15154	17057	28922	114	12430	73677

The above numbers containing seventy-three thousand six hundred and seventy-seven, is the amount of the Census within the District of Kentucky.

SAMUEL M'DOWELL, Jun.
Marshal for the Kentucky District.

NORTH-CAROLINA.

Edenton District.	Number of heads of families.	Free white males of 16 years and upwards.	Free white males under 16 years.	Free white females.	All other free persons.	Slaves.	Total free persons of every description.	Total of every description of persons.	
Chowan, including town of Edenton	556	641	559	118	41	2588	2423	5011	
Perquimons	709	885	923	1717	37	1878	3562	5440	
Pasquotank	800	951	1034	1810	79	1623	3874	5497	
Camden	583	727	758	1480	30	1038	2995	4033	
Currituck	795	1017	1024	1960	115	1103	4116	5219	
Gates	631	790	775	1515	93	2219	3173	5392	
Hertford	655	814	823	1533	216	2442	3386	5828	
Bertie	1440	1762	1841	3514	348	5141	7465	12606	
Tyrrel	709	807	959	1777	35	1166	3578	4744	
Newbern District.									53770
Cravan, including town of Newbern	1438	1709	1538	3227	337	3658	6811	10469	
Jones	581	736	794	1541	70	1681	3141	4822	
Johnston	775	1039	1119	2083	64	1329	4305	5634	
Dobbs	914	1162	1293	2478	45	1915	4978	6893	
Wayne	805	1064	1219	2256	37	1557	4576	6133	
Pitt	1088	1461	1507	2915	25	2367	5908	8275	
Beaufort	781	951	926	1824	129	1632	3830	5462	
Hyde	627	795	718	1522	37	1048	3072	4120	
Cartirett	580	718	707	1502	92	713	3019	3732	
Wilmington District.									55540
Newhanover, incl. Wilmington	629	834	695	1497	67	3738	3093	6831	
Brunswick	319	380	398	779	3	1511	1560	3071	
Bladen	635	837	830	1683	58	1676	3408	5084	
Duplin	724	1035	1187	2054	3	1383	4279	5662	
Onslow	721	828	939	1788	84	1748	3639	5387	
Fayette District.									26035
Cumberland, incl. Fayetteville	1344	1791	1557	3059	83	2181	6490	8671	
Moore	639	849	968	1570	12	371	3399	3770	
Richmond	739	1096	1205	2116	55	583	4472	5055	
Robeson	868	1131	1141	2244	277	533	4793	5326	
Samson	936	1145	1281	2316	140	1183	4882	6065	
Anson	795	1034	1183	2047	41	828	4305	5133	
Halifax District.									34020
Halifax, including town of Halifax	1405	1835	1778	3403	443	6506	7459	13965	
Northamton	1113	1334	1273	2503	462	4409	5572	9981	
Warren	802	1070	1319	2220	68	4720	4677	9397	

NORTH-CAROLINA.

	Number of heads of families.	Free white males of 16 years and upwards.	Free white males under 16 years.	Free white females.	All other free persons.	Slaves.	Total of free persons of every description.	Total of every description of persons.
Halifax District Continued.								
Franklin	809	1086	1400	2316	37	2717	4842	7559
Nash	854	1143	1426	2627	188	2009	5384	7393
Edgecomb	1260	1659	1879	3495	70	3152	7103	10255
Martin	795	1064	1009	2022	96	1889	4191	6080
								64630
Hillsborough District.								
Orange, incl. Hillsborough	1749	2433	2709	4913	101	2060	10156	12216
Granville	1165	1581	1873	3050	315	4163	6819	10982
Caswell	1322	1801	2110	2377	72	2736	7360	10096
Wake	1294	1772	2089	3688	180	2463	7729	10192
Chatham	1269	1756	2160	3664	9	1632	7589	9221
Randolph	1163	1582	1952	3266	24	452	6824	7276
								59983
Salisbury District.								
Rowan, incl. Salisbury	2492	3288	3837	6864	97	1742	14086	15828
Mecklenburgh	1741	2378	2573	4771	70	1603	9792	11395
Iredell	770	1118	1217	2239	3	858	4577	5435
Montgomery	707	967	1121	1798	5	834	3891	4725
Guilford	1093	1607	1799	3242	27	516	6675	7191
Rockingham	844	1173	1413	2491	10	1100	5087	6187
Surry	1076	1531	1762	3183	17	698	6493	7191
Stokes	1329	1846	2104	3778	13	787	7741	8528
								66480
Morgan District.								
Burke	1257	1716	2111	3685	11	595	7523	8118
Wilks	1277	1614	2252	3726	2	549	7594	8143
Rutherford	1182	1584	2145	3463	2	614	7194	7808
Lincoln	1405	2058	2294	3937		935	8289	9224
								33293
Total,	52989	69988	77506	140710	4975	100571	293180	393751

The Marshal begs leave to observe that the assistants having not returned the numbers of the different towns separate from the counties in which they were situated, renders it out of his power to make a distinct return of them, but is satisfied that not one town in North-Carolina contains more than 2000 inhabitants.

JOHN SKINNER,

Marshal for North-Carolina District.

SOUTH-CAROLINA.

Parishes.	Counties.	Districts.	Free white males of 16 years and upwards, including heads of families.	Free white males under 16 years	Free white females, including heads of families.	All other free persons.	Slaves.	Total.
All Saints		Georgetown	104	102	223	1	1795	2225
Prince Georges		do.	1345	1450	2236	80	6651	11762
Prince Frederick		do.	907	915	1596	32	4685	8135
		Cheraws	1779	1993	3646	59	3229	10706
Fairfield	Camden		1335	1874	2929		1485	7623
Chester	do.		1446	1604	2831	47	938	6866
York	do.		1350	1612	2690	29	923	6604
Richland	do.		596	710	1173	14	1437	3930
Clarendon	do.		444	516	830		602	2392
Claremont	do.		517	841	1080		2110	4548
Lancaster	do.		1253	1537	2074	68	1370	6302
Edgefield	Ninety Six		2333	2571	4701	65	3619	13289
Pendleton	do.		2007	2535	4189	3	834	9568
Spartanburgh	do.		1868	2173	3866	27	866	8800
Abbeville	do.		1904	1948	3653	27	1665	9197
Laurens	do.		1969	2270	3971	7	1120	9337
Grenville	do.		1400	1627	2861	9	606	6503
Union	do.		1500	1809	3121	48	1215	7693
Newberry	do.		1992	2232	3962	12	1144	9342
		Beaufort	1266	1055	2043	153	14236	18753
North part	Orangeburgh		1780	1693	3258	21	4529	11281
South do.	do.		1421	1478	2782	149	1402	7232
St. Phillips } St. Michaels }		Charlestown	2810	1561	3718	586	7684	16359
St. Bartholomew		do.	625	491	1017	135	10338	12606
St. Johns	Berkley	do.	209	152	331	60	5170	5922
St. Georges, Dorchester		do.	337	311	604	25	3022	4299
St. Stephens		do.	81	45	100	1	2506	2733
St James Santee		do.	140	110	187	15	3345	3797
St. Thomases		do.	145	67	185	34	3405	3836
Christ Church		do.	156	138	272	11	2377	2954
St. James Goose Creek		do.	158	79	202	15	2333	2787
St. Johns	Colleton	do.	209	104	272	22	4705	5312
St. Andrews		do.	125	71	174	31	2546	2947
St. Pauls		do.	65	48	103	15	3202	3433
			35576	37722	66880	1801	107094	249073

I do hereby certify the above to be a just return of the Census of the State of South-Carolina, as taken by my Assistants. Given under my hand this fifth·day of February, 1792.

Is. HUGER, *Fed. Marshal.*

Page 54 (reverse blank) in The New York Historical Society's copy of "Return of the Whole Number of Persons Within the Several Districts of the United States . . ." (Philadelphia, 1791).

Names of the Counties and Towns within the district aforesaid.	Free white males of 16 years and upwards, including heads of families.	Free white males under 16 years.	Free white females, including heads of families.	All other free persons.	Slaves.	Total.
Fayette County -	3241	3878	6738	30	3689	17576
Nelson - -	2456	2746	4644	34	1219	11099
Woodford -	1767	1929	3267	27	2220	9210
Bourbon - -	1645	2035	3249		908	7837
Mercer - -	1411	1515	2691	7	1317	6941
Lincoln - -	1375	1441	2630	8	1094	6548
Jefferson - -	1008	997	1680	4	876	4565
Madison - -	1231	1421	2383		737	5772
Mason - -	431	676	952		208	2267
Lexington, in Fayette County	276	203	290	2	63	834
Washington, in Mason County	163	95	183		21	462
Beards Town, in Nelson County	52	49	85	1	29	216
Louisville, in Jefferson County	49	44	79	1	27	200
Danville, in Mercer County	49	28	51		22	150
The whole amount,	15154	17057	28922	114	12430	73677

SAMUEL M'DOWELL, Jun.
Marshal for the Kentucky District.

Page (reverse blank) between pp. 54 and 55 in·
The New York Historical Society's copy of "Return of the Whole Number of Persons Within
the Several Districts of the United States . . ."
(Philadelphia, 1791).

GEORGIA.

	Free white males of 16 years and upwards.	Free white males under 16 years.	Free white females.	All other free persons.	Slaves.	Total of each county.	Total of each district.
Lower District.							
Camden	81	44	96	14	70	305	
Glyn	70	36	87	5	215	413	
Liberty	426	264	613	27	4025	5355	
Chatham	846	480	1130	112	8201	10769	
Effingham	627	336	711		750	2424	
							21566
Middle District.							
Richmond	1894	1925	3343	39	4116	11317	
Burke	1808	1841	3415	11	2392	9467	
Washington	947	1024	1885	2	694	4552	
							25336
Upper District.							
Wilks	5152	6740	12160	180	7268	31500	
Franklin	225	243	417		156	1041	
Greene	1027	1111	1882	8	1377	5405	37946
Total,	13103	14044	25739	398	29264		82548

Savannah, 25th June, 1791.

R O Bt. F O R S Y T H, *Marshal*
District of Georgia.

Schedule of the whole number of persons in the territory of the United States of America, South of the River Ohio, as taken on the last Saturday of July 1791, by the Captains of the Militia within the limits of their respective districts.

	Free white males of 21 years and upwards, including heads of families.	Free white males under 21 years.	Free white females including heads of families.	All other persons.	Slaves.	Total of each county.	Total of each district.
WASHINGTON DISTRICT.							
Washington .	1009	1792	2524	12	535	5872	
Sullivan .	806	1242	1995	107	297	4447	
Greene .	1293	2374	3580	40	454	7741	
Hawkins .	1204	1970	2921	68	807	6970	
South of Fr. Broad	681	1082	1627	66	163	3619	
							28649
MERO DISTRICT.							
Davidson .	639	855	1288	18	659	3459	
Sumner .	404	582	854	8	348	2196	
Tennessee .	235	380	576	42	154	1387	
							7042
	6271	10277	15365	361	3417		35691

Note. There are several Captains who have not as yet returned the Schedules of the numbers of their districts, namely : In Greene County, three—in Davidson, one—and South of French-Broad, one district.

September 19th, 1791.

W^m: BLOUNT.

By the Governor,

DANIEL SMITH, *Secretary.*